Letters From the Front

Poems in Trauma Recovery

Beck Duffield

DEDICATION

For my amazing illustrator, devoted husband, and partner, Christopher. For our amazing kids, Lili and Jack, and my all-grown-up stepson, Justin. Thank you for seeing me through the growth and changes I've had to make throughout trauma recovery and reveling in the slow emergence of the woman I was always meant to be.

You gave me the courage to survive, thrive, and finally publish this book.

For better or worse, you're stuck with me.

I love you with my whole heart.

Beep.

CONTENTS

LETTER TO THE READER

First, I want to thank you for opening this book. The fact that you're looking at these words at all indicates at least a small amount of interest in the works within, so I'm grateful for whatever brain space you're willing to dedicate to my rantings.

I've been told not excuse my work before presenting it, so I'm not going to do that here. I will, however, endeavor to offer a crumb of perspective.

I have quirky taste. Bordering on tacky, really. My house is full of weird things I've collected: a painted window, various tarot decks, offbeat works by independent artists, books in languages I don't read, a couple empty bottles of Chateau Picard… and among these collected bits and bobs is a sign that I received as a gift. It says, "do not be afraid of change. Be afraid of not changing."

It's my life's trajectory summed up on a $14 piece of clearance rack wood from Homegoods.

The poems you're about to read are indicative of that very philosophy. I have changed since writing them. My style, my opinions, my increase or decrease in finesse related to the particular topic being addressed. These poems were the harbingers of that change. From the first pen stroke on the first letter of the first word to the period at the end of the long-breathed sentence, change occurred. That moment of expression between the first word and the last likely brought clarity, catharsis, or both. Either of these have the power to alter perspective.

These words may not be fully representative of who I am today, but at the very least, they represent who I have grown from, who I once was, whose metaphorical bones hold up the foundations of the present.

I hope you enjoy this little peek into the cracks and crevices of my wild mind and forgive the verbosity and self-indulgence that propelled me toward the publishing of this book.

Choose love. Spread peace. Defend both.

Beck

1 A DISCUSSION OF POETRY

This piece is a confession that I often feel like a fraud. I carry many titles in life, all of which can feel false to me, but "poet" is the title that represents the struggle of the moment. It's also a bit of a warning to the reader, a preview of what's to come if you continue to journey through this book with me.

I call myself a poet

But I don't truly know what poetry is for.

Conventional wisdom says that poetry is a vehicle for expression.

It should be beautiful,

Melodic,

Emotional...

When most people think of poetry, they remember Shakespeare's comparison to a summer's day

Or Emerson's definition of success

Or Poe's tragic cries for Annabelle Lee.

All beautiful.

All melodic.

All emotional.

And none of these sound like me.

My poetry is not light,

Not sweet,

Not consoling,

But sharp,

Exacting,

And disturbing.

It is expression

But not one of saccharine love

Or observation of natural glory

Or an extended metaphor about trees,

Or poppies,

Or starlight...

It is a scream

For justice

With fading hope for the future.

It is a shout for the voiceless

And like those shouts tend to be,

It is often unpleasant to hear.

I'm not even sure it's poetry at all

But I do know that there are words that must be shared

In any medium that will hold them

And so I share them

Here

In poetry

Because maybe that's what poetry is for.

I'm not even sure it's poetry at all

But I do know that there are words that must be shared

In any medium that will hold them

And so I share them

2. THE HARDEST PART

This poem was written just as I began my journey toward trauma recovery. Anyone who has CPTSD or has been through extended trauma knows that the beginning of the recovery period is full of deconstruction. Everything you thought you knew is brought into question, every memory requiring reexamination. You lose trust in your own perspective for a while and it's intensely disorienting.

Tied in knots

Of large and splintered ropes

Constricting my every move

With guilt

Or gratitude

Or whatever it is.

Being a witless victim was so much easier

Than the accountability for healing I now place upon myself.

Growing up sucks.

Maturity is overrated.

With all the wisdom we gain

We conclude that many of our challenges

Are self-perpetuated

And not an onslaught of unfair, extenuating patterns of circumstance

Way beyond our own meager powers of control.

Shit.

I allow people to control me

To ridicule me

To make me into what they would have me be

And I used to scream

Helpless.

It was bullshit.

All of it.

I gave up the fight I pretended to engage in

At least then I looked tough.

Now, I'm all too aware of my weakness

And so is everyone else who crosses my path.

Damn it.

I dug my trench

And now I have to climb out of it

With an untrained body

And a naive mind.

A being full of nothing but ideas of what I used to be

What I should have become

What was once possible.

I'm sick of it.

Tired of being a charity case

And a pat on the head.

A pretty little thing with good manners and eloquent speech

To make someone a pleasant wifey someday

Who longed to be a badass bitch

And played the part

But never had the tits to back it up

With a mouth that wrote checks that my butt couldn't cash

And an ego unshakable

On the outside.

I don't want to pretend to be happy anymore.

Pretend to be strong.

Pretend to be tough.

Pretend to follow my dreams.

Pretend to give a single shit about any of the motherfuckers.

Wax poetic

And speak politely

And hide my temper

My opinions

My body

My pain.

First, I find my horse

And corral it

Then gather my equipment

And tack up

Next I need my courage

To help me mount,

Track the battle

And gallop into it

Waving my flag

And screaming at the top of my lungs.

Sore and jaded

Careworn and pissed off

Ready to mow down the enemy

Or be defeated with honor

Knowing I did my damnedest to reach the other side.

But first, I have to take these heels off,

Uncharacteristically high,

And shed the costumes I wear day to day,

The masks

The covers

The safety net

Fuck, its cold,

And that is a long way to fall.

But, I'm finally willing to do the hardest part;

The start.

3. MISTAKE

I was raised in a strict Roman Catholic household. I was a damn good Catholic for a while, believe it or not! I might actually be more flattered if you didn't believe it. This next poem is what it looks like when a queer feminist woman struggles under the yoke of compulsory religious heterosexual patriarchy.

Every morning, I awoke with a start.

Did my makeup slide off in the night?

Is my costume rumpled?

Has the facade broken while I slept?

I let down my guard long enough to let the nightmares in.

Mistake.

Dressing for battle,

For defense,

For the ability to hide in plain sight.

Dragon scales to cover the soft flesh,

Ashamed skin,

My only weakness,

Of many.

Readying myself to play my part,

My role,

My place in the world.

Quiet and active,

Never slowing,

Never speaking,

Never ceasing.

A work-horse that needs no stable.

A rock-star that seeks no audience.

A superhero saving the day without a theme song.

A silent servant.

And I emerge

Cursing every hair out of place,

Natural curls betraying the irons.

Picking at scabs

I created myself

So I could feel something.

Control anything.

Dodging bullets

And sneaking cigarettes

Hoping anyone gave enough of a fuck to ask what was wrong.

No one did.

I would have lied anyway.

Day after day,

Year after year,

I performed.

I pirouetted,

Pivoted,

Practiced my steps on slippered pointe feet.

A pretty little princess

Draped in pink.

Tittering submission,

A perfect accessory.

A polite laugh here,

A graceful dance there.

Sing for the man, girl.

A sweet song.

That one about the Virgin Mary, I think.

That would be best.

Not too loud.

Best to fade into the background, you know.

A chair.

An ottoman.

A rug more expensive than your dignity.

Soft and warm

Underfoot.

This is what success looks like for you.

Submission.

Service.

Silence.

Slavery.

And I tried.

I shaved off

Body hair

Blemishes

Opportunities

And pieces of myself

Just to fit.

A bloody stump shoved into the molds

Never quite filling them

But always too large.

Extra.

So much extra baggage to lose

To hide

To burn.

And the flesh grew rotten

Sores under the armor

Never exposed to the healing air

For breath or bandage

Or nourishing sun.

Stifled cries for mercy

Held down hard in the trash can

Lid sliding off.

Muscles trembling

Fighting against the righteous rage of the goddess trapped inside.

And losing the fight.

Finally.

4. LAST CALL

You know when you get that wild, anxious feeling that sends you running for an adrenaline rush or an adventure into something hyper stimulating? No? Just me? Well, this "burn the town down" feeling I used to get (okay… I still get) sent me in younger days to some really awful social situations. I knew the prevailing methods of escape from the terrors of life, but I often found most of those escapes more terrible than the terrors themselves.

Combat booted foreplay drives disgust into a generally accepting heart.

I feel like a snob today.

Clothed sex on a sweat-covered dance floor

Upon which actual dancing is rare.

Rhythm is optional and generally discouraged.

Heterosexuality is laughable. We're all a little gay.

But LGBTQIA does not directly translate to 3G DTF.

Gender is a social construct.

But folk still clinging hard to that binary.

Surreal looking people screaming for attention without saying a word.

Puke in the corner.

Piss on the staircase.

Acquaintances who avoid you.

Bartenders who ignore you.

DJs who could give a shit about what clears the dance floor.

People who cry out for acceptance practicing elitist hypocrisy.

Strange women and even stranger men grabbing my ass and smelling my hair.

What's consent anyway?

Single boys desperately fighting for the brass ring that would have fallen into their hands had they not over-reached for it.

Insecure girls measuring their value by their bra size because they were told to.

Folx in between laughing at the folly of it all.

Necessarily lowered standards.

Common ideas of normalcy deliciously reversed.

I am the star of the freak show

Feeling like a pristine schoolteacher in a hedonistic jungle of bodies and fluids thereof

Covering her eyes for some comfort.

Even the darkness is better than

The moment the house lights turn on.

5. THE WOMAN THAT WAS

That same energy that drove me through the doors of awful night clubs often drove me into the arms of awful men. This one is always tough for me to revisit because it reminds me of how little I was asking for myself.

The woman that was wanted to know you,

See every part of you,

Even the dark recesses covered in cobwebs and boobytraps.

She wanted to revel in your successes

And encourage you toward more of their kind.

The woman that was would have taken care of you

In any capacity you would have allowed

And stretched herself outside of her own comfort

To please you.

She would have danced with you

And made the other men jealous

Of what you were and what you had.

The woman that was made your parents laugh

Loved them as her own

And looked after their greatest treasure

With all the strength and tenacity she could muster.

She was giving and asked only for regard.

She tried to bring joy into a hardened heart

To soften it

And protect it

And put it back together.

The woman that was sought to be a loyal friend,

A crash pad and stepping stone,

Someone to stand beside you.

She fought with you

And inspired a depth of rage and passion you had seldom known.

She loved you

Unsure of that love's parameters.

She had the courage to let you remain undefined, floating in her life

Because she believed in you.

She believed every word you said

Took it for truth

And smiled because of it.

The woman that was recovered from one disappointment after another

Because she wanted to.

She believed the best of you

And got the worst

And she didn't want to anymore.

The woman that was couldn't take another heartbreak at your hands.

And she decided to grow

Into the woman that is.

6. CAMELOT

Trauma makes love difficult. Love without trust is nearly impossible and trust is nearly impossible for the traumatized. I wanted so badly to be seen and known and loved but I had no idea how to treat love like something other than an existential threat. When everything feels like danger, how do you know where the dangers actually lie?

Unwelcome intruders invade my thoughts

And I retreat

Scared and shaking into a dark corner in my mind

Where there are cobwebs and a dry, familiar smell

Sweat

Clenched teeth

Chewed fingernails down to the quick

Inevitably,

I grow tired of the darkness and run to the nearest patch of sunlight

And breath of fresh air

And it hurts

But I accept it

Better to feel pain than be immune to pleasure

Get out of here.

This is not where you belong.

Even after you leave, there are footprints where you stood

Mocking me

Reminding me of you

And the lack of you

And the fact that I stupidly and proudly told you to go.

My fucking temper

I can't get it under control.

"Spirited" is a nicer word.

I don't deserve it.

You make me want to create things;

Masterpieces of bittersweet longing.

And I tried to push you out again.

Why?

Your fingertips on my skin stroke more than my body.

Your voice is of a frequency that resonates in parts of my mind that lie dormant without you.

I see your soul.

I don't know how

And you hate every minute of it.

Yet,

You continue to invade

Penetrate my defenses

Without really trying

Because you get a rush or a kick out of it.

Your laughter at me makes me laugh at myself

And that's always a healthy decision.

I have very little power over you

And that pisses me off

And turns me on

And sends me reeling into a cyclone of identity crisis;

Makes me wish we could shave off little pieces of ourselves and apply them to each other.

I am my own queen

And I cannot rule you.

As a matter of fact, I believe I hardly effect you at all.

Paint the roses red and off with their heads

Falling on deaf ears and closed minds

The ravings of a crazed woman who walks the line between insanity and genius.

Or insanity and something else I can't think of

Shit.

I can't resist.

I try so hard.

It makes sense.

But sense never held much sway over me.

So be kind.

You found the knothole that opens the door to my secret entrance

And you use it

Often.

Don't abandon it now.

Don't betray it to my enemies.

Protect me half as much as you wound me and I'll survive.

The blows you deal me heal in time

And I want you on my side

To sit at my round table

Or lay me down upon it

Off of the throne I never belonged upon

In the kingdom I'd rather not have to govern.

Maybe you do belong here.

7. CATACLYSM

When the traumatized brain is insistent upon the constant presence of threat, safe places feel doubly dangerous. Because you cannot clearly identify a threat, you convince yourself that something insidious is hiding in the shadows. You manufacture threat in order to feel in control, even if it takes becoming the threat. You know something is going to sabotage your safety and happiness. If you can't figure out what's gonna do it and when, you do it yourself and quickly.

I chastise myself for thinking about you.

I can't.

I shouldn't.

I am.

I dismiss it as another passing fancy,

Ignore that it's so much more,

Deny what my body says is right,

Shut it down and turn away to focus on something else.

I can't take my eyes off you

And when yours meet mine thunder crashes in our minds.

This is electric.

This is beautiful.

This is cataclysmic.

You see me like I've always wanted to be seen.

You really see me.

You see the woman I am and have yet to become.

We dance in circles to avoid the topic at hand,

On both our minds,

And it remains unspoken.

Torturous.

Why us?

Why this?

It's not fair.

You stumble into my life exactly when I need you

But it seems I was a bit too late.

I don't want to sweep through your world like a hurricane

And blow it all down.

I was never meant to be a tempest,

The identity you won't let me escape.

I'm not sure that I want to escape this type of storm.

It feels good to be your temptress.

You're driving me crazy,

Right up the wall.

You confuse me, excite me, enlighten me, understand me,

Drink me in with your eyes,

Devour me in all the ways current circumstances will allow.

Yet, withholding pieces of myself,

I don't let you envelop me.

A cruel and strangely pleasurable twist of fate,

One of nature's little games.

I'm searching for purpose here,

Grasping at straws,

Painstakingly resisting,

Pulling myself away.

You're in my head now,

My heart.

Our souls kissed last night

And again this morning

And again this afternoon.

This can only bring us heartache.

This can only be cataclysmic.

Letters From the Front

And again this morning

And again this afternoon.

This can only bring us heartache.

This can only be cataclysmic.

8. MY MOTHER'S DOLL

While I was in treatment for CPTSD, I was told to buy myself a doll; something cute that reminded me of myself. I chose a Raggedy Anne because that's what my mother used to call me when I looked less than perfect. When examining childhood memories from a healing perspective, I was to look at the sweet little doll and ask myself if she would deserve what was said or done to me. The answer was always "no." It totally changed my perspective on my childhood and gave birth to this poem.

I was my mother's accessory.

A cute little doll she could dress however she wanted.

Paint her face.

Change her hair.

Carve her down to the right size.

The doll took orders, too.

"Stop looking so impressed," was one of the first she learned.

"Listen to this smoking cessation hypnotism tape, but every time he says 'cigarettes,' I want you to think of food."

That one worked several times.

The doll began to congratulate herself on how much hunger pain she would endure from day to day.

"But you've never missed a meal," my mother hissed at the doll.

"Fat girls eat in secret. Fat girls sneak food."

Starving girls sneak food too.

My mother stitched and unstitched her doll repeatedly. A little more fluff here, a little less there. Tried cutting her to make her shorter, but she grew despite it.

Mother dressed her doll in ill-fitting clothes, shaming her for outgrowing them. Ignoring her when she vomited from the squeeze in her jeans.

When Mother was feeling manic, she showered the doll in vestments she couldn't choose and didn't want, received after a thorough upbraiding about her appearance, her personality, her self, and how much all of it needs to change.

Her favorite Dolly play date was one that began in the car, where Dolly couldn't get away.

For Dolly's own good, my mother would tell her everything that was wrong with her.

And it was a long list.

Every move Dolly made had been weighed and measured and was torn to pieces in front of her eyes.

Dolly was often left tear-stained, red-faced, and staring blankly. Shaking, but trying to hide it.

Broken.

But Mother didn't believe her doll would dare to break.

Anyway, that's when play time would really start.

Makeup to cover the blotches.

A few outfits chosen for her because, remember what we said in the car earlier, Dolly has terrible judgement and would do much better if she would just do everything mother said.

Straighten the curls. Bleach the auburn.

Peel the skin. Wax the eyebrows. File the teeth.

Get injections.

All those needles.

Tests to diagnose growth as a sickness.

Dolls aren't supposed to grow.

My mother pathologized every move her doll made.

Pituitary problems.

Thyroid problems.

Hormone problems.

Weight problems.

Food problems.

Attitude problems.

Spiritual problems.

Drug problems.

Laziness problems.

Anything but the actual problems or the stitches needed.

She had all kinds of cute nicknames for her doll, too.

Veruca (as in Veruca Salt)

Brunhilde (this is a size and sexuality insult, not the compliment being compared to Brunhilde actually is.)

Dyke. (This one is pretty clear.)

And she recited, in a mocking voice;

There was a little girl

With a little, tiny curl

Right in the middle of her forehead.

When she was good, she was very very good,

But when she was bad, she was horrid.

She made her doll look up "horrid" in the dictionary, rather than tell her the meaning.

It sounds like my mother and the doll were inseparable, but that's not true.

There were long periods during which the doll would wonder if my mother had forgotten she existed.

She would try to get her attention; for a popped stitch or a quick hug… but my mother would ignore her for days at a time.

When she wasn't being corrected, the doll stared at the back of my mother's head, waiting for the moment she decided to turn around.

Falling asleep waiting for that moment.

Sprawled on the floor of a shit-covered office

Littered with every paper, every pen, every half used notebook my
mother ever received.

And Dolly grew while Mother wasn't looking.

She couldn't help the growing

And she tried.

And then

One day

She just didn't fit in the dollhouse anymore.

9. SELF PORTRAIT

If you treat someone like garbage for long enough, they start to believe they belong in the trash can.

There's something missing in this room.

It needs to be long

And unobtrusive.

Something that fits in the corner

And fades into the wallpaper.

A piece of furniture to fill the space.

We can throw darts at it.

We can cast it knowing glances.

We can take everything it has.

Knock it over

And tell it to thank us when we prop it back up

Just to get it out from underfoot.

These are new shoes and I'd hate to scuff them.

We need an inanimate object

With no feelings

and no voice

No tears to speak of or draw out

Silent and still.

A conversation piece in its absence

Or rather, when its absence is noticed

Which it seldom is.

We can bump into it and never apologize.

Shit, we can break it in half

and laugh when it can't piece itself back together.

Or we can pretend it never happened,

That the object broke itself.

There's definitely something missing...

Or maybe I'm just imagining it.

10. DREAMS OF FLIGHT

This piece chronicles the intoxicating lightness of the darkest moments. Sometimes the flight entices you away from the fight, but never forget that the battle can still be won if you stick around long enough to claim your victory.

I'm closer than I've been in a long time

Staring down into the uncorrupted air

Where gravity becomes everything and nothing

Weightless

Light, dark, and completely free

Naked and breathing deeply

Full expansion of the lungs

A brand new journey into a place I've only imagined

Un-temporary (yeah, I said it.)

The wind kisses my face and teases me

Beckons me to come

To follow the fluttering leaves and debris

To fly

To fall

It's inevitable eventually

Why not now

When at least one person will notice

Will witness

Will care

Will miss me when I go

11. THE ACTRESS

Turns out masks aren't reserved for the theater.

All I see is a facade

The show you put on for everybody else

You dress up in your costumes

And your makeup

And your expensive shoes

And hope everyone sees you

And fear anyone seeing you.

12. TO ERR IS HUMAN

Deconstruction is a terribly uncomfortable process. You have to unbecome everything you were built to be in order to become what you actually are. It's often demoralizing and can leave you feel like you're weaker than what the moment demands. You're not.

I wish I was a good girl

But I'm just not.

I thought I was

But I was wrong.

I thought I was a poet, too

Turns out I'm just verbose

But people will buy

If you sell skillfully

And I do.

I wish I was a goddess

But I'm just not.

I thought I was

But I was wrong.

I thought I was captivating, too

Turns out I'm just attractive

But people are drawn to

What is stronger than they are

And I am.

I wish I was a fighter

But I'm just not.

I thought I was

But I was wrong.

I thought I was a fortress, too

Turns out I just look like one

People accept well-crafted facades

And I have one.

I wish I was liberated

But I'm just not.

I thought I was

But I was wrong.

I thought I was innovative too.

Turns out I was only trying to be

But my effort's not wasted

If I make people feel safer

And I do.

I really thought I was a poet

But I was wrong.

13. THE MAN FROM THE DINER

One of the many jobs I took while scraping for independence was as a waitress in a local diner. There, I met The Man. Like me, his life had given him more than enough reasons to be jaded and bitter. However, also like me, he was determined to keep laughing, keep smiling, keep sharing what little joy he had to spare. He was a big feeler and a heavy heart. Flames that burn that bright tend to burn out quickly, and sadly, we lost him far too young. For what little time we had to enjoy our friendship, I truly loved this guy.

He was lost.

No matter where he stood

He was lost

Because his predecessors were lost.

The people meant to guide him through this life until they could no longer stay in it.

Hopeless, depressed, without direction.

Two junkies raising another.

Passing the bottle, the blunt, the needle,

The blind leading the blind

Baby with the bathwater.

He had no concept of right and wrong because they didn't.

He had a good heart and a big brother who never should have borne the responsibility of raising him.

He got really really crossways sometimes.

Head heavy with grief and worry

They were convinced it was going to kill him

But this lost little boy had a man to grow into.

He had laughs to share and love to receive

And he found that love in me and mine.

We laughed with him.

We loved him

And he grew into the man he was supposed to be.

Then

Just as he arrived

He was gone.

His heavy head so lightened that it carried him away

Beyond us

Beyond reach

Beyond this life that weighed him down.

And there he sits.

At last.

Found.

14. FATHER'S DAY

Now that we're on the subject of untimely death, I may as well go ahead and address the elephant in the room.

My father left this world in May of 2015. I was very attached to him in a way I now know to be trauma bonding. There was a lot about that man that was monstrous, but I was devastated to lose the person I believed him to be at the time. This is one of the many ways I memorialized that grief.

Dad left me a voicemail when I was too busy with my kids to pick up the phone.

"Hey, Beck. It's Dad. Just give me a call when you get a chance. Nothing urgent. Love ya. Bye."

Nothing urgent, he said.

When you lose someone you love, it doesn't get easier. You just get more time between the hard parts.

So, I returned his call.

"Hey, Bean!"

It was a nickname my family gave me.

It was the only casual thing he said.

When you lose someone you love, it doesn't get easier. You just get more time between the hard parts.

With a quiver in his voice, he told me he had the flu.

He apologized for being too sick to make it to my upcoming graduation.

He told me he was proud of me.

That I was among his greatest accomplishments.

That all his life's boxes had been checked off because of me.

Because of who I am.

When you lose someone you love, it doesn't get easier. You just get more time between the hard parts.

He told me he loved me and he promised to rest.

I asked if I could help and he refused.

I thanked him for his unfailing encouragement, his unfailing love.

And we hung up.

I didn't like the tone in his voice.

I called my mother and asked if I should come over.

She said, "No. Dad needs to rest."

I had a bad feeling all night.

I ignored it.

I took my family out for hamburgers and we watched my favorite reality show.

I should have gone.

Why didn't I go?

When you lose someone you love, it doesn't get easier. You just get more time between the hard parts.

Around 7:30 the next morning, the call came.

My mom. Crying so hard I thought she was laughing.

Wailing. Screaming.

"Daddy's dead! Becky, he's dead!"

"Stay put. I'm calling 911 and I'm on my way."

"Marietta, GA. My mom thinks my dad is dead. No, I'm not there yet. Please send someone."

Streaks in my eyes. No idea what I'm wearing. Flurries of diapers and baby shoes. Car seats. Traffic. Screaming at the traffic.

Having to tell my husband that my father died on his birthday.

I don't remember the drive.

When you lose someone you love, it doesn't get easier. You just get more time between the hard parts.

Somehow, I got both kids inside.

The police and the coroner beat me there.

But they weren't wrestling two toddlers.

My mother, more composed than I expected, but less composed than I'd ever seen her,

Informed me that the police officer wouldn't allow me upstairs

And that he knew my uncle Tommy.

Blurs. Streaks. Hugging Mom.

Setting the kids up to play and watch television.

Still not understanding.

I decided I'd waited long enough.

Fuck the coroner.

That's my father up there.

I marched up the stairs against my mother's warnings.

"He's not wearing pants and there's a mess."

"I don't care."

When you lose someone you love, it doesn't get easier. You just get more time between the hard parts.

His eyes were open.

His mouth dotted with foam-

His last breath frozen in time forever.

His feet hung off the bed.

He was a tall man.

But he was paler now.

There was a mess.

The stillness after a storm.

Stagnant. Impossible.

He knew he was dying.

It was all over the room.

Evidence. Tells. Spots. Blur.

The stillness. Impossible.

When you lose someone you love, it doesn't get easier. You just get more time between the hard parts.

I spoke to him.

"Hey, Dad."

Like he could hear.

Like he could reply.

Then the switch flipped.

My brother called it "business mode."

Cleaning the room. Consoling my mother.

"I should have checked on him. I heard him coughing."

"You just wanted him to rest."

Then the depths came loose.

"I should have let him off the hook." Sobs. Collapse.

Holding up the woman who held me as a baby.

"Go downstairs, Mom. I'll handle this."

"He wouldn't want you to see him like this."

"I got it, Mom. Go sit down."

My brother arrived to help me dress Dad.

"Oh, Dad. Dad."

Frozen. Tried to close his eyes. It didn't take.

I made jokes about changing diapers. Told Dad not to be embarrassed.
I handled this kind of stuff all day.

I laughed. I smiled.

What the fuck.

Choosing clothes. Lifting stiff legs.

Giving Dad his dignity.

I cleaned his body.

When you lose someone you love, it doesn't get easier. You just get
more time between the hard parts.

I couldn't let the morticians cover his face.

He was claustrophobic. Like me.

I couldn't let them cover his face.

Father John led a prayer.

"His face says 'Oh, God! My God.' Gary was called home by the
Father. He saw the face of God in his final moments."

An attempt at comfort when all I saw was fear.

Blurs. Watery streaks.

The phone calls. His office, the funeral home, his family, his friends.
My siblings.

What do I tell the kids?

He was a big man.

It was a challenge getting him down the stairs.

His ears were blue from the rush of blood.

But don't cover his face. He's claustrophobic. Like me.

I didn't know it was the last time I would see him.

Ever.

Last touch.

Last squeeze of his long fingers.

Never again.

Never.

When you lose someone you love, it doesn't get easier. You just get more time between the hard parts.

Organizing. Planning.

Calls. Papers. Schedules.

What do I tell the kids?

Husband arrives. Is that really the time?

Forgetting to eat.

Never sleeping.

Too many sobs for sleep.

Too much stone to eat.

Too much to do.

We bury him soon.

Blurs. Streaks. Sobs. Panic. Frozen solid and numb.

Pretending to function.

Pretending to be in one piece.

Shattered. Lost. Adrift without anchor.

Breaking people's hearts one phone call at a time.

How do we go on?

One thing at a time.

There's nothing we could have done to save him.

Choosing boxes.

Arranging music.

Calling priests.

Receiving guests for hours and hours.

The most well-attended wake I'd ever seen.

Anger welling. Throwing things.

Too many cigarettes, too few minutes to cry.

Taps.

Photos.

The hole is too deep.

We can't just leave him here.

Hours sitting alone at the grave.

Blur. Streaks. Tears.

When you lose someone you love, it doesn't get easier. You just get more time between the hard parts.

Hours. Days. Weeks. Months.

Have to be better.

Not better yet.

Holidays. Festivals. Inside jokes. Voice messages I can't erase.

The smell of his clothes.

His footprints.

His car.

Text messages.

Old cards.

Photos.

He's gone.

I can't believe he's gone.

Explaining to my two-year-old that we can't go see Bub because he's with the Angels.

She asks when he'll get back.

"What's wrong, Mommy? Mommy's crying?"

"I just miss Bub, baby. That's all."

"We'll go see him! In the car!"

She doesn't understand.

I'm glad, but I don't want to explain it again.

"He's flying with the Angels, baby. With Jesus and Mary."

"Ohhhh, okay! Nudder crackers please!"

She doesn't understand.

Neither do I.

Tests.

Jobs.

Life developments.

Needing a word, a hug, some encouragement. From him.

And finally, a tattoo. Over my heart.

Three checked boxes.

"All my life's boxes are checked off because of you. Because of who you are."

Check.

Check.

Check.

Over my heart forever.

And slowly, I move on.

Have to be better.

Not better yet.

When will I be better?

Not now.

Not ever.

When you lose someone you love, it doesn't get easier. You just get more time between the hard parts.

Just more time. That's all.

15. DECLARATION OF INDEPENDENCE

The anger stage of trauma recovery is real. Sometimes you've just gotta get pissed off and tell folks how it's gonna be. Author's Tip: Try reading this one aloud like a monologue the next time someone acts like they know your experience better than you do.

Here it is folx,

My personal Declaration of Independence.

This is not

A charge into war with a tyrannical government

An uneducated F-You to the establishment

Or even an angsty, pubescent "yer not the bossa me" to self-important authorities.

This is a bulletin

A broad announcement to anyone who gives a shit and even those who don't

TO SERVE NOTICE

I refuse.

Yup. I said fucking REFUSE

To be baited

To be brought down

To be disappointed with you who didn't deserve my faith in the first place.

I refuse to let another day be ruined by someone else's pissy little fist-pounding hissy fit not even a mother could love.

I've decided to point and laugh instead.

I will never let you make me doubt myself ever again.

Yea, you. The one who tries to convince me that I'm toxic, damned for all time, never going to be the shining bastion of success and morality you have cultivated in yourself.

GET

THE FUCK

OUT OF MY HEAD

Your nagging little voice doesn't mean anything to me anymore.

ATTENTION:

ALL FALSE PROPHETS, JEALOUS RABBIS, IMPIOUS PRIESTS, AND CLOSETED, SELF-LOATHING EVANGELISTS ARE HEREBY SILENCED AND BANISHED FROM THE KINGDOM.

THAT IS ALL.

On the other hand (I have more refusals to talk about)

You will no longer affect my faith in mankind.

You will not destroy my ability to trust.

You will never NEVER steer me away from my chosen path.

Your insecurities about who got there first, who made it work and who didn't, who's busting ass and who's not, who has had more help, who has earned it and who hasn't, who gets more attention, who has more money, who buys more expensive clothes, which side of the fence has greener grass...

Not my problem anymore.

Work that shit out your damn self.

My only concern is my happiness, the family I have made for myself, and leaving a better world behind than the one I arrived in.

Oh! There must have been some misunderstanding!

'Cause I don't see MAINTAINING YOU anywhere in there!

No mistake.

Read it. Absorb it. Commit it to memory, bitches.

I have been so accommodating.

I have eaten more than my fair share of dirt.

To please you.

To placate you.

Until the next time you decided to be a pain in the ass.

I tried.

I tried so fucking hard that it hurt me.

And now

Guess what

The cowtow machine, the automatic bootlicker, the one-stop-shop for all your punching-bag needs has just hit the guard wall.

It's totaled.

Too bad.

Yup. That means exactly what you think it does.

I HEREBY RESIGN FROM MY POST OF WHIPPING BOY.
TWO WEEKS NOTICE WILL NOT BE GIVEN

BECAUSE I COULDN'T CARE LESS ABOUT YOU FINDING A
REPLACEMENT. I DON'T EXPECT REFERENCES EITHER.

THANK YOU.

FUCK OFF.

END TRANSMISSION.

In conclusion,

I hold these truths to be self-evident

I am going to be the best person and live the best life I can.

I'm going to succeed

and I don't give TWO SHITS

about subversive opinions on the subject.

This is me.

Take it, leave it, whatever.

I depend on no one to determine my worth.

I rely on no one to cultivate my happiness.

I make my own.

I am my own

And I will never be anything of yours

Ever again.

This is my declaration of independence.

I hope you fucking choke on it.

65

15. NO TRESPASSING

Anger is extremely uncomfortable to confront. My pain was so whitehot sometimes that it would really tax the energy of the people around me. Sometimes that taxation of energy forced them to step back in a practice of self-preservation. I can't blame them. It was consuming me, too. However, there was no escape from the anger for me. The only way out was through.

I'm a little tough to get close to.

I'm not gonna lie.

I'm that bitch whose body cries out for physical contact but is also a total germaphobe.

(I was that way before the pandemic made it cool.)

Low key obsessed with personal hygiene.

Shitty, right?

Snobby?

Hypocritical?

What you don't know is that body odor is a panic trigger for me.

Memories of being forced to hold the snot-crusted hands of strange men while saying the Our Father.

Memories of the man who stopped the funhouse ride to molest me in the dark on my 13th birthday.

Memories of the beer-breathed rapist who didn't take a push and groan as enough protest from semi-conscious woman.

Memories of unwanted visitors in the night.

I won't apologize for the consequences of actions taken by others.

I'm that bitch who always has eloquently worded advice and encouragement to offer.

And I will never ask you to return the favor.

Even though I desperately, *desperately* need the support.

What you don't know is that asking for help was conditioned out of me from birth.

Cries silenced.

Bodily cues ignored.

Genuine distress invalidated.

Emotionality ridiculed.

Righteous anger punished.

Vulnerability exploited.

I'd shoulder the fucking world on my own if I could.

And you'd have to talk me out of it.

I'm that bitch who just wants to feel like she belongs and cannot help but change every space she enters.

I don't know what to be if I'm not leading.

And I'm SO TIRED of leading all the time.

What you don't know is that submission to nearly any authority immediately puts my body in crisis.

Authorities have only ever betrayed me.

As hard as I try to please.

If I'm not in charge, my body tells me I'm in danger.

Because I often am.

I am not a great leader.

And sometimes, it's all I'm capable of being.

I'm that bitch who always looks like money but barely has any.

Whose ability to fake having it together is so well practiced that people resent her calls for aid.

Surely they're struggling harder than I ever have, right?

What you don't know is that my estranged mother is a mentally ill shopaholic who needed to offload regretted purchases onto me in justification of her compulsion.

Then, she used all that offloading as a manipulation, calling me ungrateful for not shitting myself with joy over crap I never asked for and didn't want.

You think I would have chosen that ugly ass backpack for myself? But, it's Vera Bradley, so I MUST be grateful.

Her need to purchase was the point, not whether I had even the slightest interest in receiving.

It sat in her closet, untouched for three years. She didn't buy that shit for me.

But I use it. Because I won't spend the money on another one until this one gets a hole in it.

I'm so spoiled.

I'm that bitch who will turn up her nose at food you're serving or the restaurant you picked.

Who won't go to that bar with you unless there's live music or it's karaoke night.

Who orders coffee and water at that bar.

Who leaves early and encourages you to call a cab instead of driving home.

What you don't know is that I have an autoimmune disease and I'm neurodivergent due to PTSD.

This makes me tired, skittish, hyperaware, shitty in social situations, and allergic to damn near every food and drink on the planet.

I'm hungry, I'm thirsty, I'm overstimulated, I'm exhausted, I'm getting a headache, my ass is bleeding, my joints hurt, I'm masking heavily, I'm constantly scanning for predators, I'm probably scared, and the smell of alcohol makes me want to barf.

And I miss my husband and kids.

And I'm cold.

I love you so much and you are heaps of fun but I have to go home now.

I know I'm a little tough to get close to.

But please believe me when I say

I'm so happy when you try.

15. EYELESS

An eye for an eye makes the whole world blind. Is there anyone with vision left? I wonder sometimes.

How do I convince you to care about other humans when you don't even see them?

You won't look at them.

Look at us.

Those people you labeled "over-sensitive" have survived horrors I don't even wish on you when you judge them.

Judge us.

Those pesky complaints, little razor-edged arrows pin-pricking your good time until you're getting a little uncomfortable here....

We are uncomfortable.

We live uncomfortable.

Neither you nor your forefathers knew what it meant to be an object for consumption.

To be the property of men who look like you;

The esteemed owners of women who look like me

And anyone who looked like anything else.

It didn't stop a long time ago.

It didn't stop with emancipation.

It didn't stop with women's suffrage,

It didn't stop with integration,

Prison letters from humanitarian poets,

The projected voices of great preachers dying for our sins.

It didn't stop with burning crosses,

Or Spousal Rape Immunity.

It didn't stop with the trans murder defense.

With toothless hate crime legislation,

Total ignorance of femicide and sexual assault statistics,

Employment discrimination based on gender expression,

My black and brown bodied siblings getting shot by their own police....

Will it ever stop?

How do I convince you to care about other humans when you don't even see us?

And you say you stand for justice. For freedom. For equality.

You tell me how many times you've tippy run to your car in heels you never wanted to wear in a skirt that cut into you all day with three layers of covering over the same fucking nipples your boss uncovered at the company pool party because you have a creepy coworker who likes to follow you out and tug your hair while asking if you've been a good girl over the weekend while blowing his goddamn whiskey breath on your neck.

Tell me how many times you've weighed losing your income against punching the man who won't stop giving you unwanted shoulder rubs at your desk.

You tell me how many generations of free men there are in your family.

Tell me how far you can trace your roots. Do you know your great great grandmother's original last name?

You tell me how many neighborhoods your parents were turned away from because of a "no-coloreds clause" or a "traditional families" clause in an HOA agreement.

You tell me how many times you've been threatened or assaulted because of the color of your skin or your sexual orientation or gender.

How many times you've been told to speak a certain language or get the fuck out.

How many times your family has been slaughtered and robbed of their ancestral homeland and then told to be grateful for the trailer park full of smallpox blankets and alcoholism they were handed in return.

How do I make you care about humans you don't even see?

Refuse to understand?

Whose stories are too depressing r too woke for your taste.

If they were straight, white men, would you care?

Do all victims deserve to be silenced for harshing your buzz or is it only the ones who don't look like you?

The ones you don't see.

16. IN GOD'S COUNTRY

From blindness to clear vision... a major part of my recovery was the deconstruction of religion in my worldview. More and more, the abuses of religion and the hypocrisy of the religious became glaringly obvious when viewing them through healing eyes. At the time this piece was written, the United States was (and still is) wrestling heavily with white christofascist nationalism on a frightening scale. Hopefully, by the time you're reading this, that philosophy has been firmly set down and is an ugly and repugnant thing of the past.

In God's country, poverty is a myth.

In God's country, racism doesn't exist.

In God's country, every neighborhood is your kind of neighborhood.

In God's country, you can pronounce everything on the menu and converse easily with the waitstaff.

In God's country, everyone knows the lyrics of "The Devil Went Down to Georgia."

In God's country, everyone stands for the same flag, sings the same songs, holds the same hats over the same hearts.

In God's country, there's always a cold beer waiting for you at the end of a long day. Or the beginning of one. Or both.

In God's country, Sundays are for church and football.

In God's country, the only tattoos are military symbols and bible verses.

In God's country, everyone is armed to the teeth.

In God's country, your kids would never dream of deciding to be gay.

In God's country, your son gets his ass kicked for wearing a dress to prom.

In God's country, you'll drop a $20 in the plate but call the cops on the homeless.

In God's country, you exploit cheap immigrant labor then vote to have them deported.

In God's country, women know their place and men know how to keep them there.

In God's country, school children go hungry while choking on bullets, thoughts, and prayers.

In God's country, this is a Christian nation founded on Christian principles like slavery and homophobia and misogyny.

In God's country, family members are cut off for leaving churches and speaking truth to abuse.

In God's country, no one goes to gay weddings even if the brides and grooms are sons and daughters. There wasn't any cake anyway.

In God's country, girls are raped because of what they wore or what they drank. They should have covered up and known better.

In God's country, businesses get to pick and choose who to serve or fire for any reason.

In God's country, publicly funded entities have religious affiliations and discriminate based on them.

In God's country, boys get their first beer with Dad by the lake at 13. They grab wings at Hooters afterwards.

In God's country, the wife needs to remember who the head of the damn household is.

In God's country, you say grace in public.

In God's country, hijabs must be removed for identification purposes.

In God's country, there's a cross in the classroom but books are banned.

In God's country, they erect statues of traitors and murderers in the town square because they're distant relatives of ours and they really did have a point.

In God's country, they name parks after slavers so everyone remembers how much weight those tree branches can hold.

In God's country, they make their daughters take purity pledges at 12.

In God's country, they don't believe their daughters when they accuse family members of molestation. Just cover up when Uncle Joey comes over and there won't be a problem.

In God's country, they torture queers to save their souls.

In God's country, wives and mothers build entire personalities around getting wine drunk as often as possible.

In God's country, songs praise Jesus and drunkenness and cut-off jeans in the same sentence.

In God's country, unhappy women are sent to bible study and then divorced for not looking slutty enough.

In God's country, men will stuff a dollar into a stripper's G-string, but won't give her a chance to interview for a job at the companies they run.

In God's country, poverty is a choice. Charity should only be given to animals or churches.

In God's country, every other God is lie but yours is 100% real.

In God's country, ten-year-old girls are forced into motherhood because it was God's will that a child be raped by a grown man. Maybe they should just get married.

In God's country, high school students learn what death rattles sound like while hiding from gunshots under their desks.

In God's country, queer boys are dragged behind trucks and left tied to trees in fields to die.

In God's country, judges are concerned about ruining the lives of promising young rapists.

In God's country, rapists sit on the highest bench in the land.

In God's country, chemical-laden fast food is affordable and growing community vegetable gardens on sidewalks is illegal.

In God's country, they sell diet plans to the abusive mothers of eleven-year-olds and watch them starve, permanently damaging their developing brains in the name of thinness.

In God's country, they praise their sons for their sexual conquests and shame their daughters for the same.

In God's country, sexy women are sluts and all other women are bitches. There's no in-between.

In God's country, their governing philosophy is a document written in the 1700s by slavers and misogynists who didn't believe most members of the current population were people at all.

In God's country, they invade a kingdom, overthrow it, outlaw their language, imprison their queen, and then accuse them of putting on their culture for the tourists who ruin their land.

In God's country, they rob peoples of their ancestral homes and push them into a diseased trailer park on the least farmable land possible.

They should be thanking their government for the accommodations and the tax breaks.

In God's country, men and women were hanged and burned for knowing which plants could cure a toothache or soothe a sunburn.

In God's country, citizens are murdered by their own police force. The murderers walk free for months before the mildest consequences possible are exacted.

In God's country, corporations report record profits while households report record struggle.

In God's country, you're not owed a living wage for full time work. You're lucky to have a job at all.

In God's country, the rich deserve everything they have and the poor deserve to starve.

In God's country, one illness is enough to bankrupt a family for generations.

In God's country, "now remains faith, hope, and love, but the greatest of these is love."

In God's country, no one should wear masks or take shots or stay home to save the lives of others. You haven't had a tall boy with the Applebees regulars in days.

In God's country, anyone who steps on your property gets a gun pointed at them.

In God's country, anyone who isn't white takes the bullet.

In God's country, burning crosses merge into blue lines.

In God's country, infants are measured in terms of "domestic supply."

In God's country, the poor and the sick aren't allowed to vote.

In God's country, children perish from deadly viruses in cages because they were born on the wrong side of an invisible line in the sand.

In God's country, Mary carries her fourth iPad because, dammit, she keeps dropping them, while Martha has to share the one library computer that serves her entire high school. And they call this equal educational opportunity.

In God's country, public bathrooms are locked because homeless people don't deserve access to toilet tissue and soap late at night.

In God's country, kids watch their friends overdose on drugs because they're afraid they'll go to jail for life if they call for help.

In God's country, it's illegal to feed the poor without a permit.

In God's country, theocrats are called terrorists as long as they are brown.

In God's country, tyrants are called dictators as long as they aren't white.

In God's country, imperialism is a gift to the weak from the strong.

In God's country, they say "give us this day our daily bread" and refuse to pay workers enough to feed their families.

In God's country, your right to carry a gun is more important than my kid's right not to be killed by one.

In God's country, a woman's rapist can sue her for aborting his baby.

In God's country, coaches demand genital checks for all their female athletes.

In God's country, entire generations bond with their parents through plexiglass.

In God's country, kids recite the pledge, "one nation, under God, indivisible, with liberty and justice for all," before they're old enough to realize that every word is an outright lie.

In God's country, those children are only protected until they're actually born.

In God's country, people line up and do what they're told.

In God's country, we stop resisting.

In God's country, we can't breathe.

In God's country, godliness left a long time ago.

19. METEMPSYCHOSIS

Starting fresh in trauma recovery is extremely disorienting. For me, it felt a bit like I had been liberated from a cult that, up until that moment, defined my place and perception of reality in every possible way. Having to deprogram that and look at the world with fresh eyes felt like a second adolescence of sorts. I wasn't sure what I liked, what I wanted, who I was, because I didn't have the space to discover all of that when it usually naturally occurs. I skipped the individuating stage of adolescence entirely and had to clunk into it, fighting for every inch, as an adult. I'm still struggling against the cocoon a bit, but the gap in the wall is wider than it has ever been.

The reemergence of being.

Not a crossroads or a precipice

Reached on a journey

From one point to another.

Not at all.

Leaving the road completely.

The laws of traffic, gravity, and mass tonnage

No longer applying.

Rejecting them.

And it takes.

The light changes

Illuminates, exposes.

Shadows shift, protest, and flee.

Burning hot enough to melt, liquify

And sanitize.

Floating sideways.

Drifting beyond control.

Disciplined hands kept from thrusting out against the spin.

Powerless to resist

But not powerless.

Not ever again.

Comforted by discomfort

As proof of life.

Not many have the constitution for antigravity.

But dizziness runs in the blood.

This is nothing.

Floundering in a shallow pool.

Feet finally found.

Stinging with the chemicals of cleanliness

Hearing the silence of drowning unnoticed

And opening the drain.

Washing away.

Washing clean.

Then reemerging to begin again.

20. PROMISES BEFORE MOTHERHOOD

One of the most important discussions I had to have with myself was deciding what kind of mother I wanted to be. It's a difficult task while defining who you are outside of what you have been told to be. Thankfully, I found that defining myself as a parent helped me tremendously in defining myself as a person. Sussing out my parenting philosophy told me massive amounts about who I am at the core. These are the promises I made my babies.

Your tears will never annoy me.

I'll never make you feel crazy for your emotions.

You'll have all the hugs you ask for and even ones you don't.

And I'll leave you alone when you want me to.

I'll start your days with smiles.

Your home will be filled with love.

I will assure you every day that you are the most beautiful gift to my life.

You won't feel ugly.

You won't be ignored.

You won't be called names.

Stupid, fat, worthless, self-centered, dramatic, whore, inconvenience, disgraceful...

The list goes on

Of things I'll never say to you.

You'll always be welcome in my heart and my home.

I won't judge you for your inevitable phases.

I'll never be ashamed of you.

Because you'll be part of me.

As much as I'll always want you near me, I'll let you go where the wind blows you

And visit as much as I can

And write

And remind you that I think about you fondly every day- every moment.

You'll never be the butt of my jokes.

You'll never be my penance for sins of my past.

I'll always be on your side.

I'll try my hardest not to tell you what you should have done

When the moment's already over.

When I lose my temper, I'll apologize.

I'll never raise my voice for no reason.

Your home will be free of chaos and adrenaline and fear.

I will help you pursue your passions

And give up my own comfort to do so.

I'll volunteer as makeup designer for your plays, booster club member for your sports, host your parties... or none of these if you prefer.

I'll buy enough fundraiser crap to get you the prize you want.

I'll do my best to get you the clothes and music and whatever you need to be one of the cool kids, but I'll make sure you stay true to yourself and remind you that the coolest kids are the kindest kids.

I'll help you apply for colleges.

I'll teach you how to shave your legs or ask out crushes.

I'll teach you manners and presentation so you'll go far in life.

I'll encourage you to be healthy, but I won't condemn you for choices I disagree with

And I'll never use the gifts I give you as a weapon.

I'll be firm when you when you need it and you'll understand why.

I'll save up to get you expensive treatments when you have acne.

I'll take loving care of your pets when you're away.

I'll take you out dancing on your 21st birthday.

I won't interrupt you or make you feel like your words are annoying me.

I'll let you pick the decor for your bedroom- with a little influence, of course.

I won't judge your friends unless they hurt you.

I will always tell you the truth unless its inappropriate.

I'll do my best to understand that the path I would have you take isn't always the one that will make you happy.

I'll drive you and your friends wherever you want to go whenever I can.

I'll give you chores to teach you responsibility.

I'll reward your successes.

Barring unavoidable circumstances, I'll be at every sporting event or show that you do

And I'll always tell you that you were wonderful- even when you mess up.

You will never be the subject of malice or jealousy at my hands.

I'll make sure you know that you can tell me whatever is on your mind.

When you ask me for help, I will give it to you.

I'll pick you up when you're drunk and thank you for not driving.

You'll know all about sex before it is sprung upon you.

I'll answer any question you have and not make you feel stupid or insolent for asking it.

When I decide you cannot do things that could potentially harm you, I'll provide you with equally fun alternatives.

I'll drive you to prom in the coolest car I can get my hands on.

I'll never embarrass you in front of your friends; at least, not on purpose.

I'll give you all the freedom you show me you deserve.

You won't be afraid of me being in your life.

Only if I believe you are in danger will I read your journal, and I won't hold anything you write against you.

 I understand that journals are therapy, not reality.

I will not snoop through your things to satisfy my curiosity- I'll trust you to tell me all I need to know.

I'll help you with your homework and make sure you have the best science fair display we can muster.

I'll take you out- just you and me.

I'll love you no matter who you choose to become and make sure you know that every moment of your life.

I won't make you eat things you hate, but I will make you try them.

I will never EVER put you in the garbage can.

I won't make you wear clothes you feel stupid wearing.

I won't make you get involved in activities you despise.

I'll help you make educated decisions about your belief system, and respect it even if it differs from mine.

I'll let you wear blue nail polish if you want.

I'll let you dye your hair funky colors while assuring you that you're enough as you are.

I'll find your budding talents and give them the nurturing they need to grow.

I'll teach you how to ride a bike.

I'll turn off the TV when you want to talk to me.

I'll always prioritize your needs.

And most of all

I'll do my best to be a loving example for you and assure you you're always safe with me.

Until you arrive, I love you already.

21. MY KIND OF WORLD

Sometimes the only way to distract yourself from how shitty the world can be is to concentrate on the world you hope to bring about by your presence in it.

I grew up in an environment where it was unsafe to be seen.

Children need to be seen. Need to be validated and reassured.

Getting my needs met became an extreme sport.

Made me an adrenaline junkie.

Without my knowledge.

This is what the world looked like to me.

There was one way to be. The right way.

I wasn't that way. They all knew it.

The more I tried, the more they called me "desperate."

I was desperate.

Without my knowledge.

This is what the world looked like to me.

Taught the rules of the game. Their game.

Discipline. Repetition. Manipulation.

Practice, practice. Until I drop. Unconscious practice.

Gold medals, certificates, applause.

For the person they built

Without my knowledge.

This is what the world looked like to me.

I was prepared for a cruel world.

I was not prepared for a kind one.

Looking over my shoulder. Measuring my words. Assessing my posture.

Ready to strike at the first sign of trouble.

Never forgetting the eyes

The never-blinking eyes that stare and analyze

And undermine

And humiliate

And use

Without my knowledge.

This is what the world looked like to me.

I was a fool. Made a fool of, rather.

I was young. And I had a right to be.

And this cruel world I was prepared for opened its arms to me and said, "come. Let me show you your people."

And they found me before I found myself.

They knew me

Without my knowledge.

This is what the world became for me.

Like a stray who had never known safety, I remained wary.

Still ready to strike at any moment.

Prepared for the cruel world.

Kindness was met with interrogation.

"What do you want from me?"

Never staying long. Never saying it all.

Never being worth the effort to keep. To chase.

Because I wanted it that way

Without my knowledge.

This is how I moved through the world.

I tried to escape the dangers I believed were ever-present

In every way but actually escaping them.

I ran from unfamiliar safety back into familiar danger

Thriving on fight and flight

Giving everything to a few and nothing to most.

Everything was demanded and was never enough.

Why would anyone else be satisfied?

I wasn't satisfied. They convinced me I should have been.

Without my knowledge.

This is what the world looked like to me.

An ant contemplating an elephant. Only shown a small fraction of the whole.

Well prepared for a cruel world. Well rehearsed. Well versed.

And passing with flying colors.

Not my colors.

Feeling the pang of self-treason and calling it the devil.

A cancer to be cut out.

An annoyance to be ignored.

"You're too nice. That's why you're like this. Just remember that nice people burn in hell, too."

(That's a direct quote, by the way.)

And this cruelty was coded deep in me, preparing me to exist in

And to help create

A cruel world

Without my knowledge.

But, I know what the world looks like now.

I finally figured out that I get to choose what kind of world I want.

I get to choose.

I choose a world where we stand to support one another.

Standing ovations.

Standing up.

Standing with.

Standing for.

Standing together.

I choose a world that turns the volume up on the silenced and down on the hateful.

I choose a world with open arms, open doors, open hearts.

I choose a world where abundance is shared and hunger is abolished.

I choose a world where hopelessness is pursued and defeated like the insidious enemy of humanity that it is.

I choose a world where no one ever wonders if they are loved.

If they are worth being kept,

If they are worth being pursued.

I will help create this kind world.

And I will prepare my children for it.

22. MEA CULPA

I'm of the firm opinion that most of us, especially women, apologize far too much. This piece became my vow to combat this insidious piece of patriarchal programming.

I've spent too much time writing apologies for others

In my mind

And accepting them as if they were uttered by the intended actor instead of scrawled to life by the scratching of my own pen

The repetition of my thoughts

The denial of my reactions

The lies we tell ourselves to survive.

I've birthed golden-threaded scripts fit to heal decades of wounds in only a few perfectly placed words.

From a rolling line of hums thumped on an upright bass to a tinkling tickled melody plucked from the hair-thin strings of a gilded harp.

I know how to apologize.

I've done it my whole life.

Apparently, it's what I was born to do.

I've woven litanies of apologies;

Well-owed, sincere expressions of regret and desire to improve.

I've apologized for tiny missteps and massive mistakes.

I've apologized for breathing too loudly.

I've apologized for walking by someone.

I've apologized to mannequins in shopping malls.

I've apologized for having ideas.

I've apologized for genuine reaction to heinous abuse.

I've apologized for taking up too much space while flying coach

AND apologized for not being able to afford first class where asses like mine are far more appreciated.

I've apologized for speaking the truth about my life because that truth makes them uncomfortable. It's offensive to exist sometimes.

I've apologized for my age.

I've apologized for my gender.

I've apologized for my sexual and relationship orientations.

I've apologized for being friends with a man who was going through a divorce.

I've apologized for being friends with a woman right before she felt strong enough to demand one.

I've apologized for being a better boyfriend than your shitty ass boyfriend.

I've apologized for being a better girlfriend than your shitty ex wife.

I've apologized for needing a robe that fits because I'll get arrested if I let my boobs hang out at the spa.

I've apologized for having absolutely huge feet.

I've apologized for apologizing.

I've apologized for existing.

I've apologized for nothing at all.

Compulsively

Always apologizing.

Sorry about that long list, by the way.

But a some of those apologies,

A lot of those apologies

Were necessary

Were owed

Were real and genuine

Words from my heart instead of taps on a high-hat

With a rhythm all their own.

I am often sorry

As I often ought to be.

However,

This is fair notice.

I'm closing up shop.

I am no longer in the business of Professional Apology Composer.

You will no longer reap the benefit of words you never said to me,

Qualities I only imagined you had,

Intentions I intended on your behalf,

Concerns that couldn't concern you less.

I'm retiring from the apology industry.

You're gonna have to write your own from now on.

You'll have to demonstrate your care,

Follow through on your good intentions,

Express your concern,

Prove your quality,

Without the aid of my bass and harp to sing them for you.

My fingers are tired and calloused and scabbed from decades of unceasing practice

Apologizing to myself

For you.

And I set myself free from that workload today.

As of now.

As of never ever again.

23. DEAR WOMAN

How do women fight the patriarchy? Lift up other women.

Dear Woman,

You have days when you feel like the world is yours
Until the night falls.
You have moments when you think, "Damn, lady! How did you get so
fine?"
Then you squeeze yourself into a school desk designed for someone
with half your lusciousness
And you feel like the world doesn't fit you anymore.
Woman, you have days when you feel invincible
And days when you wish you were invisible.
We ALL have those days.

Dear Woman,

If I could turn myself into a magic mirror
And show you the beauty that is obvious to everyone but you,
You would never cry again.

Dear Woman,

You are made of the same material as a lioness,
As a starburst,
As a raging river.
You are made of the same elements as music,
As poetry,
As laughter.

You are magic.

Dear Woman,

You are loved.
Anyone who lets you forget that fact doesn't love you enough to really
love you.

Dear Woman,

You are beautiful.
You are a mess.
You are a storm and a breeze,
A ray of sunlight and a blaze.
You are everything you should be
And much much more.

Dear Woman,

You are strong.
You are soft.
You can be and are absolutely both.

Dear Woman,

There's no force in this wide world that can stop you.
The curve of your hips is a perfect seat for a beloved child.
The lilt of your voice is comfort and instruction.
The grace of your hands brings healing and breaks glasses.
The touch of your lips is a blessing to all who feel it
Without qualification.

Dear Woman,

Hold up your head.
Walk upright and with long steps
Because you're going somewhere.
You are a force.
You take up space.
That space is YOURS.

Dear Woman,

Don't draw another breath without taking in the support of your sisters.
You are wholly your own and we love you for it.
Your time is precious.
Your heart is gold
And your love is a priceless jewel that must be hard earned.

Dear Woman,

I lift you up in love and praise because you deserve it
Because you are who you are
And what you are.
Perfect as you are

And everything you should be.

24. UNCALCULATED RISK

When love looks like a minefield, accepting it for yourself is an act of tremendous courage.

I would rather risk my heart

Take a chance that it may be smashed to bits

Almost completely but never beyond repair

And love someone to the tips of my fingers

With everything I am

Than live with the regret

Of things that might have been

That I passed over

And defended myself against.

Having a safe heart

Immune to attack

Is much more secure

And creates a loneliness

Much more harmful

Than outside assault could ever be

Because its self-inflicted

And I know just what weapons to use

To cause the most damage.

I've practiced

And my skills are honed.

Some people jump off cliffs

With rubber bands tied to their ankles

To feel flight

For just a moment.

Some people ingest poisons

Nature never intended for human consumption

To touch death

So their lives no longer depress them.

Some people throw caution to the wind

With feats of unabashed bravery

To make waves

In our fragile little waters.

I choose the most dangerous path.

The greatest adventure.

I choose to open my heart

With passion unashamed

To grasp life

As it was meant to be lived

Without fear

Without regret

To love.

Am I safe?

No.

Will I regret this uncalculated risk?

Never.

111

25. YELLOW LIGHT

Trauma recovery is a really strange process. Once you're able to drop out of adrenal activation, you start to realize exactly how anxious you were before you began recovery. Triggers are discovered, faced, managed as best you can. Some of them can be overcome through exposure or therapeutic untying, but others remain written into your DNA for the rest of your life. Those are the ones that might lose strength but will never fall. Please trust me when I say, those permanent triggers are surprisingly few. A massive amount of recovery is absolutely possible for even the most traumatized, most hopeless soul. Never give up.

Beware of falling triggers.

They can be so strange, so seemingly innocent.

The headphones I received as a 30th birthday gift

They were a trigger today

After ten years of use.

The first chill in the air after a long Georgia summer

Comes every year.

Every year of my life.

Almost 40 years.

Still a trigger.

Tan hands with big rings and fake nails.

The smell of cigarettes and Southern Comfort.

Old Spice.

Mustaches.

Catholic churches.

Estee Lauder, Brighton, and Vera Bradley.

Brooks Brothers, Ashworth, and Joseph A. Bank.

Softball fields.

Twizzlers.

Sink holes.

Tighty-whities.

Pavarotti.

Predators.

Fast food.

Diet culture.

Pantyhose.

Suicide.

Golf courses.

Lunch meat.

Alarm clocks.

Computer screens.

Gloria Estefan.

When it's your entire life, it's everywhere.

Could be anywhere.

So, what do you do when there's fear-conditioning associated with your whole world?

You can't hide. Hiding is a trigger.

You'll probably start with an attempt to drown it out.

Be louder than the abusers.

Faster than the chasers.

Scarier than the monsters.

Tougher than your triggers.

You'll scream and yell and perform backflips and comedy routines for applause.

Execute beautiful choreography without breaking a sweat because it's easier than freestyle.

You'll shine your borrowed light brightly

An imitation of glitter

Carefully curated

Painstakingly practiced

Second nature

Controlling the input by controlling the output

Because this is how you succeed.

Right?

This is how you should grow.

Prune yourself into a flawless bonzai

Diminutive and adorable enough for the kitchen window.

A facsimile of greatness

In a palatable package.

You'll never worry about your triggers

Because you'll ignore them.

Withstand them.

For a while.

But, caution! Plants outgrow their pots when roots begin to spread.

Roots are a trigger.

You MUST grow in the pot.

You MUST fit on the table.

You MUST bend and twist and snap with the will of the shear-holders because if you don't who are you?

The wilderness is a scary place for a little table tree.

So, you'll cut roots as soon as they form.

You'll stay planted shallow with a deathgrip on inadequate soil.

Unbalanced.

Unsupported.

Undernourished.

Until you break the pot or fall.

But we mustn't break our pots.

We should be grateful for them.

They give us a place to belong.

Right?

The twist is that surviving destruction made you hearty, whether you cut roots or not.

And the remedy for destruction was just destruction in disguise.

You're surviving that, too.

Dammit.

You'll finally realize that trimming yourself to size,

Jamming yourself into a pot,

Will destroy you faster than fear.

Faster than the triggers and all their effects.

Faster than the destruction this remedy should remedy.

The remedy for destruction that is destruction itself.

You'll cast it off

And tumble naked into the wilderness. Timber!

Free of the pot and a place to belong.

Disconnection mistaken for freedom.

Then comes treason.

Without your direction

Without your consent

Your roots will know where to go.

They will dig deep by instinct

Seeking nourishment

And you'll only be able to pull them out for so long

Before you taste the sweet earth and give in.

Finally being served what should have fed you all along.

Angry at the past for withholding and angry at the present for offering.

Triggered by your own healing.

A necessary paradox.

A true remedy.

Triggers will fall.

And like an autumn leaf, you'll examine them.

You'll watch the need for survival give way to true color with the fading green.

And the truth will be beautiful

And a little sickly at times.

26. LEAN

It's horribly unfair that those in trauma recovery seem to leap from one fight to another; from the "fight" that traumatized us to the fight to survive in its aftermath. Victory seems impossible at times.

In stories of great battles, we read about acts of incomparable valor, unshakeable courage, indisputable strategy. The battle for trauma recovery requires moments like these sometimes.

Not all the time. Not most of the time.

When you're too tired for acts of valor, and you will get tired, acts of mere survival will do just fine. The victory is the same.

"Keep moving forward," they say.

"One step at a time," they say.

One step.

It seems so simple.

Yet, when you're knee deep in the mud, sinking in the quicksand, cemented to the ground....

One step can be nearly impossible.

So, a step may not be manageable.

A step may be too much.

Lean.

Just lean in the direction you want to go.

A tiny move.

A breath in and out.

A shift in weight.

Just lean.

Every centimeter traversed is a victory

And your breath, your voice travels that much farther.

Just a lean.

Toward the Eiffel Tower.

Toward a garden patch.

Toward a brighter, stiller, moment.

Toward a cleaner breath of air.

Lean.

Once.

A little further than you thought you could.

Releasing the vacuum binding you in the bog.

The air escapes and the chains are loosened.

Just a touch.

A hair.

Enough to get somewhere.

Enough to change your view.

A little wiggle room.

Just a simple lean.

Then another.

Then another.

No matter how long it takes to push the sand aside, you can always lean. Just a little. And a little more.

Progress of microscopic proportions is still progress.

You will free yourself a bit at a time.

And a lean becomes a shift.

And a shift becomes a lift.

And a lift becomes a step.

And a step becomes a walk.

And a walk becomes a sprint.

And a sprint becomes the means by which you catch up to your dreams.

Your freedom.

Just a lean.

In this moment.

It's all you need.

27. SIMON OF CYRENE

The proper support is critical to the recovery process. Forgive the religious metaphor, but even Jesus needed to hand off his cross for a minute on the way to Calvary.

Through my recovery, I had a team of Simons willing to bear some of the weight of my fight with me. Therapists, doctors, friends, mentors… but the strongest of these allies was my husband. He saw me at my absolute worst, in the moments I was too ashamed to share with anyone else. He picked up all my broken pieces every time I shattered and got straight to work gluing me back together again. Without his steadfast love and unshakeable commitment, I'm not sure I would have survived this process.

Strange.

So many assumptions I made in my youth turned out to be wrong.

Strange.

Thoughts of unquestionable truth were lies with intricate backstories.

Strange.

I never saw it coming.

Strange.

I couldn't have predicted my present position if I tried

And I'm exceptionally creative.

Strange.

Just when I lost my love for myself, someone else found it and took up its maintenance through my exhaustion.

Strange.

When he gave it back to me, it didn't split in two- it just doubled in size so we could share equal parts.

Strange.

I was not where I wanted to be and the journey there seemed too long to travel alone.

Strange.

As soon as I realized this, I found someone to go with me.

Strange.

I don't believe in "taking up crosses" but I do believe in my Simon of Cyrene.

Strange.

The things I knew were for me are not

And the things I knew I'd never have are those I am most comfortable holding.

Strange.

I have become myself; the woman I was afraid to be.

Strange.

I have no idea why I feared her vulnerability and passion.

They are what make her beautiful.

Strange.

My myriad contradictions all work towards common goals.

Strange.

I probably won't know the common goal until I reach it.

Strange.

Baby steps may actually get you somewhere.

Strange.

Here I am, the faithless, taking leaps of faith.

Strange.

That's the best word to describe it.

Strange.

And knowing what feels familiar to me, I wouldn't have it any other way.

28. THE DEWDROP

One of my most comforting thoughts in recovery was that nature creates life where it is supportable and needed. Fungi spring forth to convert poisoned soil into consumable energy. Flowers open to bees in need of nectar. Trees create oxygen for breath and shelter for life. All of this happening spontaneously. Sometimes the purpose for existence is existence itself. (Also, don't miss the reference to my precious babies, Jack and Lili.)

I was born a dewdrop on a rosebud

Nature's symphony played by moist air and morning sunshine

The conceptual made corporeal

Manifested for the creation of beauty

For the conversion of oxygen to carbon dioxide

To kiss boo-boos

To occupy space

To play with Jacks and gild Lilies.

I was born in fulfillment of nature's highest need

To fully and simply exist

Where I am

To fully and simply be

What I am

And to perform those duties to the best of my abilities.

I was born in the crashing of particles

Destruction of the past making way for a bright future

A cacophony giving way to perfect stillness

A starburst in the dark

An earthquake in the ocean

A tiny hurricane birthing the droplet that scatters the light in just the right way.

I was born with a purpose. With a place. With a destiny.

And none of me

Is anything

Controlled by anyone else.

29. AND A HAPPY NEW YEAR

Once a traumatized person drops out of permanent fight-or-flight, there's a temporary decrease in distress tolerance. We've stripped off the armor of adrenaline and now we have to face the world in the nakedness of true vulnerability. Plato's fella emerging from his cave, the light that seems so normal to everyone else can be blinding to us for a while. Like the lobster who has grown too large for her shell, we also must hide under the rocks until we shed the old and grow a new one. We will never heal if we keep exposing ourselves to the sharks.

The isolation seems daunting in the beginning. It's supposed to be sad to let go of people, right? It is sad sometimes, but it will absolutely shock you how relaxing it can be to take your head off that swivel. Especially for the holidays.

I'm actually looking forward to Christmas.

Not the pretend version of looking forward;

That manic, frantic, slightly panicked dash about wherever you are, squealing and screaming like Buddy the goddamn Christmas Elf.

Not that hair pulled, veiny eyed, twitching insistence that everything be absolutely. Fucking. Perfect.

I'm not playing the role of strung-out Christmas Mommy dancing a duet with her bestie Jack Daniels before snuggling up with a few Xanax way too close to sunrise.

I'm not pretending to be Pinterest proper with my peanut butter and chocolate chip cookie technique.

Gingerbread gets really boring after a while. I know Santa feels me on this.

I'm not biting my nails to the quick, stressing and squeezing the last few pennies I have out of my bank account in order to participate in the inevitably disappointing and unfailingly dumbass white elephant gift exchange with colleagues whose salary doubles mine.

Hope that tin of Dollar Tree hot chocolate didn't set you back too much or threaten to spill in the backseat of your Tesla, Mr. Popped Collar Executive Mullet in unironic patterned shorts and top-siders without socks.

You get nothing from me. Not even a ball jar of Bisquick with a bow on it.

I

Am doing Christmas

In my pajamas

Dammit.

We're going out for Sushi on Christmas Eve. We'll eat way more than seven fishes.

We got gluten free donuts and a pre-made ham for Christmas Day. All I gotta do is whip up some veggies and we're gold.

I'm not going anywhere I don't wanna go.

I'm not doing anything I don't wanna do.

I'm not having any conversations I don't wanna have.

I'm not pretending to give a shit about gods I don't believe exist.

I'm not having to bite my tongue while I watch religions and cults of personality turn once conscious, wonderful people into raging bigots who believe they're on the side of righteousness.

I'm not having to NOT bite my tongue with those folks.

I'm not gonna take another one on the chin and another one and another one and another one just for the sake of peace and harmony over the holidays.

I'm not schlepping packages full of shit I couldn't afford to give to people who won't appreciate it.

I'm not abiding to anyone's schedule but my own.

And, well… my kids', of course. No way I'd wake up before sunrise on Christmas if I didn't have to.

Christmas Eve, my family will gather around our fireplace in our jammies and I'll read them The Night Before Christmas.

We'll set out peanut butter and chocolate chip cookies for Santa, candy canes for the reindeer, and my kids will snuggle up in their own beds, ready for visions of sugarplums.

They won't sleep, but they won't dare come out of their room. They mustn't scare Santa away!

Christmas morning, long before dawn, my kids will wake up in their own beds and hold their hands in front of their faces until they can see the outline without the aid of a lamp.

The moment their fingers reveal themselves from the darkness, they'll bound down the hall to the master bedroom

Where I will be wrapped in the arms of the person I love most in the world.

Snuggly and warm.

Yawning and stretching.

And they will jump on our bed until we drag our old bones down the stairs to make sure Santa came.

Coffee in hand, donut holes laid out for rumbling tummies, we will give our babies the okay to put on their robes and scurry down the stairs.

And we will watch their eyes grow wide with surprise and wonder.

We will watch them jump and squeal for joy.

In our pajamas and robes.

By our fireplace.

In our home.

On our time.

Safe.

Warm.

Comfortable.

Celebrating this Christmas.

Our Christmas.

Together.

None of the dance, none of the stress, none of the obligations and expectations…

None of that could ever be better than this.

30. DAWN

Ignoring the pain of the past is the chosen road for most traumatized people. They refuse to recover because recovery requires facing your experiences, admitting how those experiences affect you... "trudging through the mud," as I often referred to it in therapy. Most folks want to sweep it under the rug and pretend the house is tidy rather than giving it the deep cleaning it deserves.

Facing your trauma is difficult. I won't lie about that. It's dirty, emotionally trying business and it's hard work. However- I know this sounds strange to say, but the act of facing the horrors of your past reality only shines a light on how much you have to be grateful for in its aftermath. The present moment shines in a way that the adrenaline would not have allowed you to thoroughly embrace. Revel in it.

I wish you a morning like this one.

Sun streaming through half-drawn curtains

The only alarm to rouse you.

Awakening in the arms of your soulmate

Stirred by the sneaking, bouncing giggles of the masterpieces both of you made.

I wish you fluffy blankets

Scrunched up noses

Wiggly snuggles

And whispered requests for breakfast and permission to play video games.

Yes to butter and jam and a firm, "not until your schoolwork is done."

Daylight bringing laughter,

Reminders of duty,

Rumbling tummies,

Professions of affection,

And secret, sideways glances at a tousled lover.

I wish you all of this.

Fresh coffee and rainbows on the floor.

Cozy couches,

Slippered feet,

Cooking sausages with a yawn.

More than enough for everyone.

More than anyone could truly wish.

Riches enough for the most resplendent queen.

With a little cream and sugar.

31. REQUIESCAT IN PACE

In this piece, I wanted to share one of the most recent developments in my recovery. We've made our way through denial, confusion, anger, isolation, and acceptance of the present moment. Now, we'll examine the ability to look back on the life you lived, dotted and smeared with challenge and trauma, and pull out those bright spots, those self-affirming moments.

Eventually, when you emerge from the hurricane of change and realization and renewal, you'll realize that the person you've become is the person you were all along. And you'll love her.

All those days

Sitting in fields with a notebook

Writing poetry

Nowhere to be

Until tomorrow.

I wish I had known how fast those days would go.

The loneliness I should have taken for serenity

The unbearable isolation in rooms full of people

As evidence of how extraordinary I was.

I was wrong to wish them away.

I wish I had known.

Endless coffees with milk and sugar

Never getting the shakes

Or crashes

Or gas.

God, the gas…

All the calories consumed and burned just as quickly

Complicated choreography done without so much as a twinge or an ache.

Sleepless nights leading to more sweet memories than miserable weeks ahead.

I wish I had known how fast those days would go.

Moving in crowds

Dancing with strangers

Screaming the lyrics to a song I'm only pretending to have loved all along.

Moving towards the noise instead of away from it.

Walking through cities late at night with my head held high and my door keys between my knuckles

Mascara running down my face.

Countless dangers on ill-advised adventures.

I didn't know.

Leaving footsteps all over strange cities in foreign countries

Traveled alone.

Unafraid and unashamed.

Standing atop waterfalls I climbed myself.

Riding horses through wild countrysides.

The flutters of new infatuations.

I think I'm glad I didn't know.

Still carrying that notebook.

Still aching to write poetry in open fields

In foreign cities

On ill-advised adventures.

Tattoos and cigarettes.

Too many cocktails and not enough time.

I never knew how fast those days would fly.

But now, I know.

I'm too old and too smart and too seasoned to make the same
mistakes,

But oh, how I long for the adventures that accompanied those
mistakes.

And I remember them

Fondly

And I know they are a part of me

And no one can take them away.

32. FINALLY HOME

What does home feel like to you?

When I first met my husband, I was baffled by the fact that home was his favorite place. I always wanted to be out, away, busy, engaged, covered in noise and activity and distraction. I ran ran ran and never rested. "Home" was a four-letter-word.

I didn't realize that I was attempting to escape the war zone. I couldn't sit still for too long or I would be captured or wounded or killed. I had no home even when I had one. Home required safety and I never felt safe.

After a good while into my recovery, we were finally able to purchase our first home together. A modest but beautiful house almost as old as I am in a town we love. Once we moved there and settled in, I finally started to realize what home should feel like. It quickly became my favorite place as well.

Home.

My favorite espresso sipped from a well-beloved mug. It's got one of those spots for your thumb on the handle. It's awesome.

Home.

A hammock chair in the chimed breeze, swaying in time with an abundance of branches.

Home.

Snoozing in the Sunday morning sunshine, wrapped in the arms of the people I love best.

Who love me best.

Home.

A balm for a battered soul.

Home.

A foreign feeling and a refuge sorely needed.

Home.

A heart warmer. A life saver.

Home.

Full bellies and fond memories of deliciousness past.

Home.

I never knew it could be this good.

Home.

Fresh air. Roaring fires. Hot baths. Cool breezes.

Home.

Giving birth to imagination in the greatest safety I've ever known.

Home.

Healing comfort. Warm embrace.

Home.

My slippers are there. And that particular cloth I like to use to clean my glasses. It's sitting right on my desk. Right where I left it.

Home.

I've never wanted to return so badly.

Home.

I've never wanted to escape from it less.

Home.

I've never known a place like this. A love that sees every corner of me, every messy pile of unprocessed junk, every quirk, every need, and jumps for joy when it sees me pulling in the driveway.

Home.

My beautiful, blue teapot reflecting the flickering firelight, sitting within easy reach of my cozy chair and fluffy blanket.

Reading to my children, snuggled up before bed.

Dancing in the kitchen.

Singing in the shower.

Decorating gingerbread.

Dispensing magic kisses and drying tears.

Crying tears

Of joy

For home.

OUR home.

I'm finally

Finally

Home

MENTAL HEALTH RESOURCES

You never have to struggle alone. Please don't hesitate to reach out to a professional when you or someone you love needs help.

National Suicide Prevention Hotline:

1-800-273-TALK (8255)
If you or someone you know is in crisis and would like to talk to a crisis counselor, call the free and confidential National Suicide Prevention Lifeline. TTY users should call 1-800-799- 4TTY (1-800-799-4889). You can talk to a counselor 24 hours a day, 7 days a week. Call the Lifeline:

- To talk to someone who cares
- If you feel you might be in danger of hurting yourself
- If you're concerned about a family member or friend
- To find referrals to mental health treatments and services in your area.

Always call 911 if you are in an immediate medical crisis.

The Trevor Project

The Trevor Project is specifically geared to aid in the mental health of the LGBTQIA+ community.

www.thetrevorproject.org/get-help/

Text START to 678-678

Call 1-866-488-7386

ABOUT THE AUTHOR

Beck Duffield is a lot.

Wife, mother, stepmother, business owner, political activist, possessor of multiple academic abbreviations, singer, actress, Survivor enthusiast, absolute nerd, and (hard though it is to admit) poet. Beck is a survivor of Complex Post Traumatic Stress Disorder and Anorexia, as well as battling more than one chronic illness. This book is a snapshot of recovery's genesis and Beck hopes to inspire recovery in others by releasing it. Her mission is to show the readers how messy recovery can be. Thereby, having witnessed these sloppy moments, those in the thick of battle will stop judging themselves and feel less alone.

Stay safe out there, friends. Keep fighting the good fight.